Calm the C*nt Down

An Irreverent Adult Coloring Book

By

S.B. Nozaz

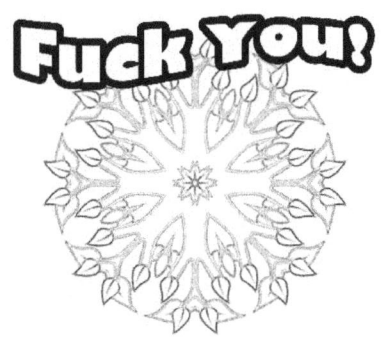

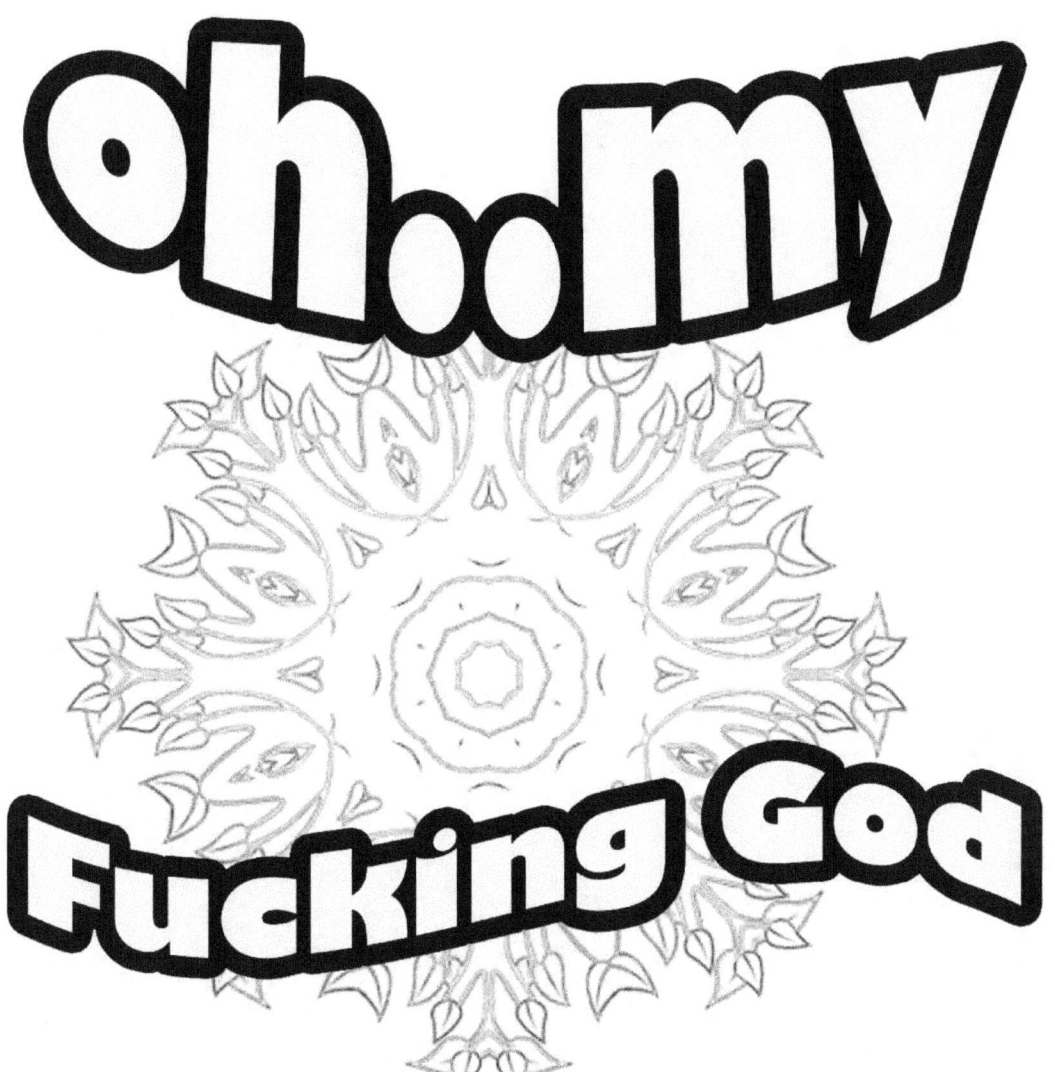

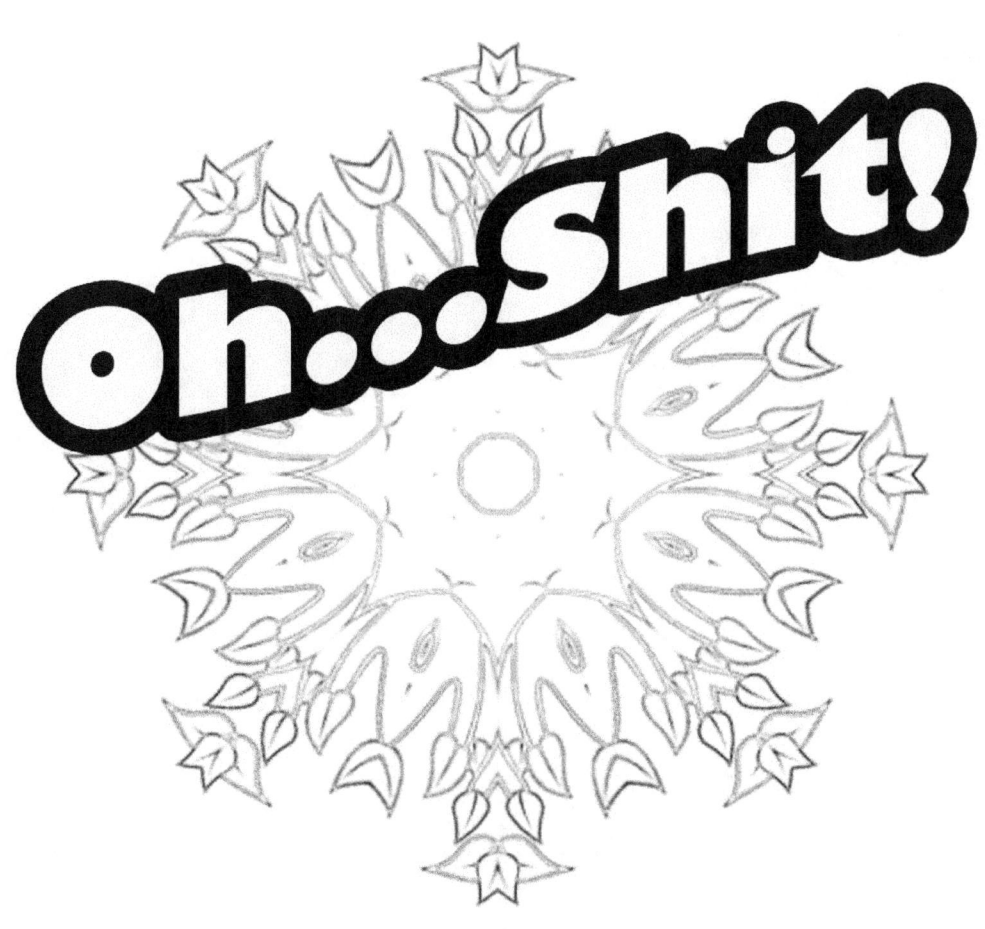

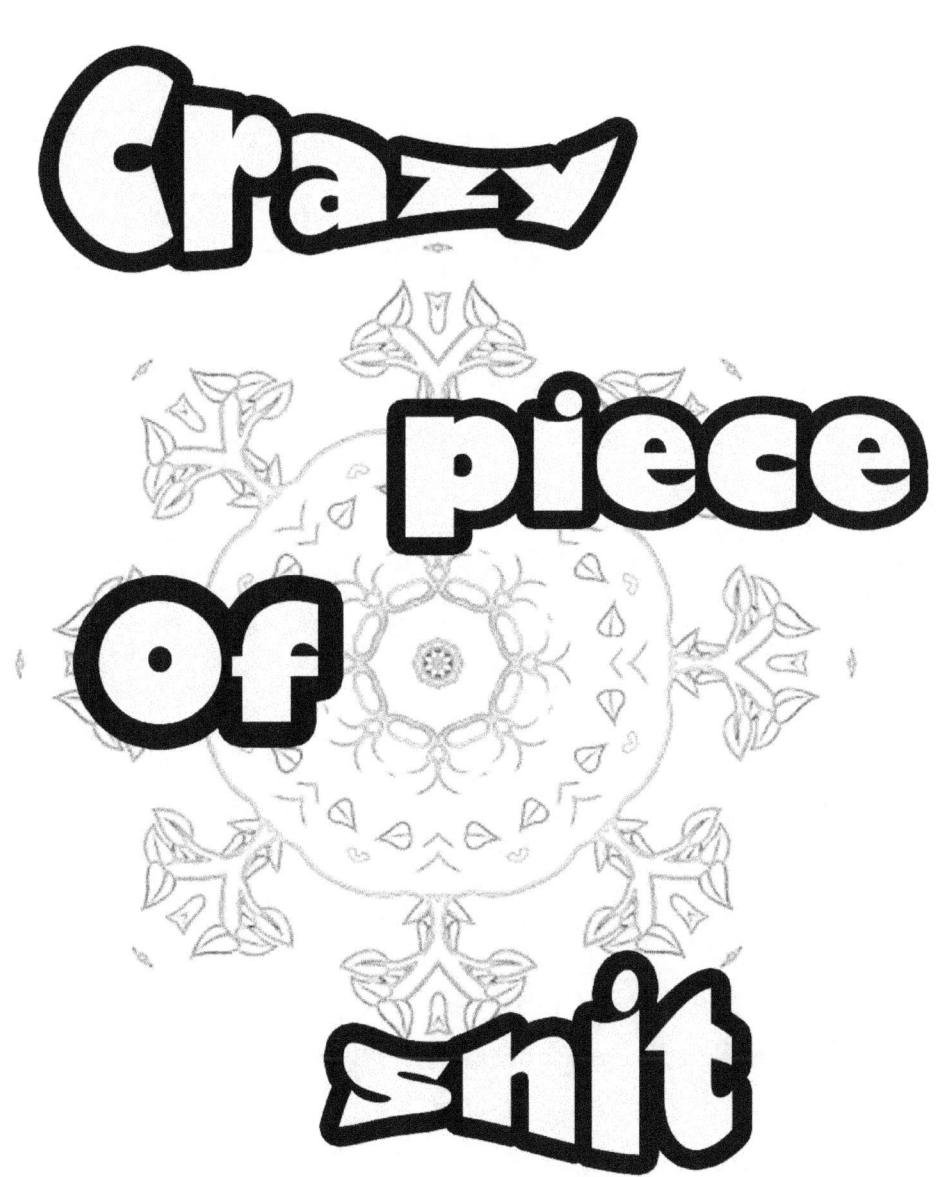

Crazy piece of snit

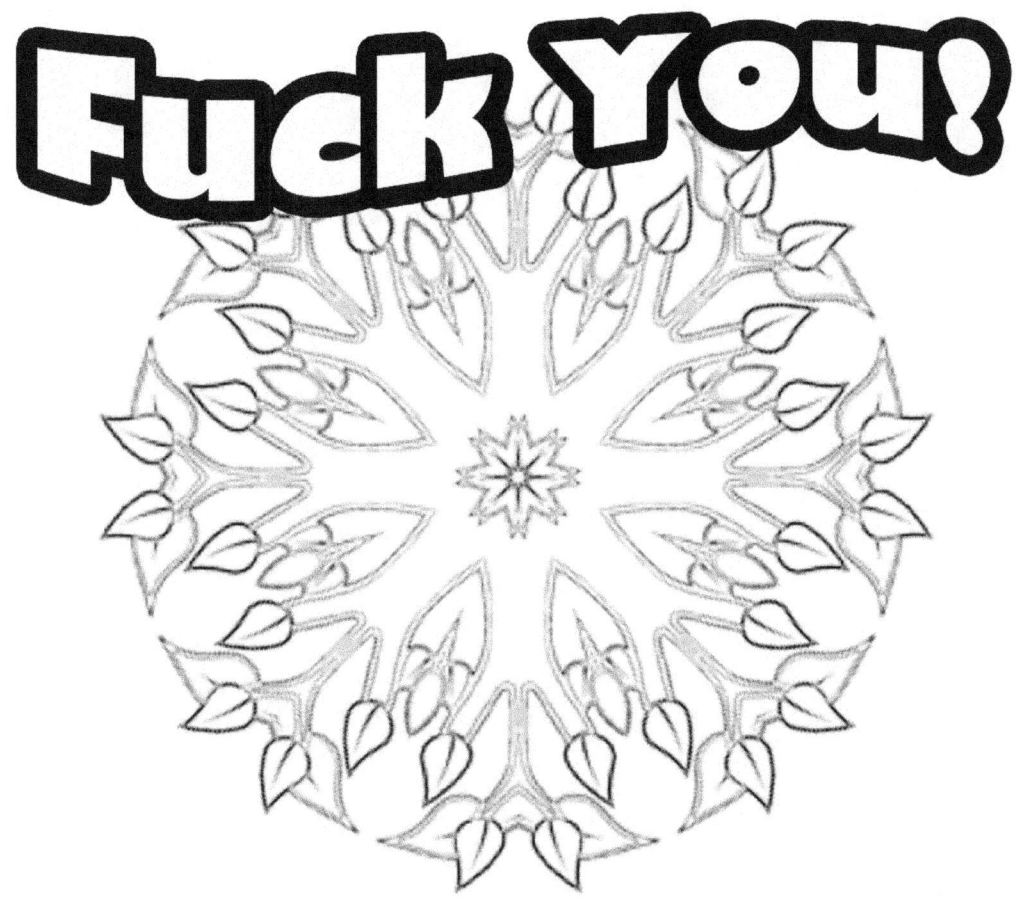

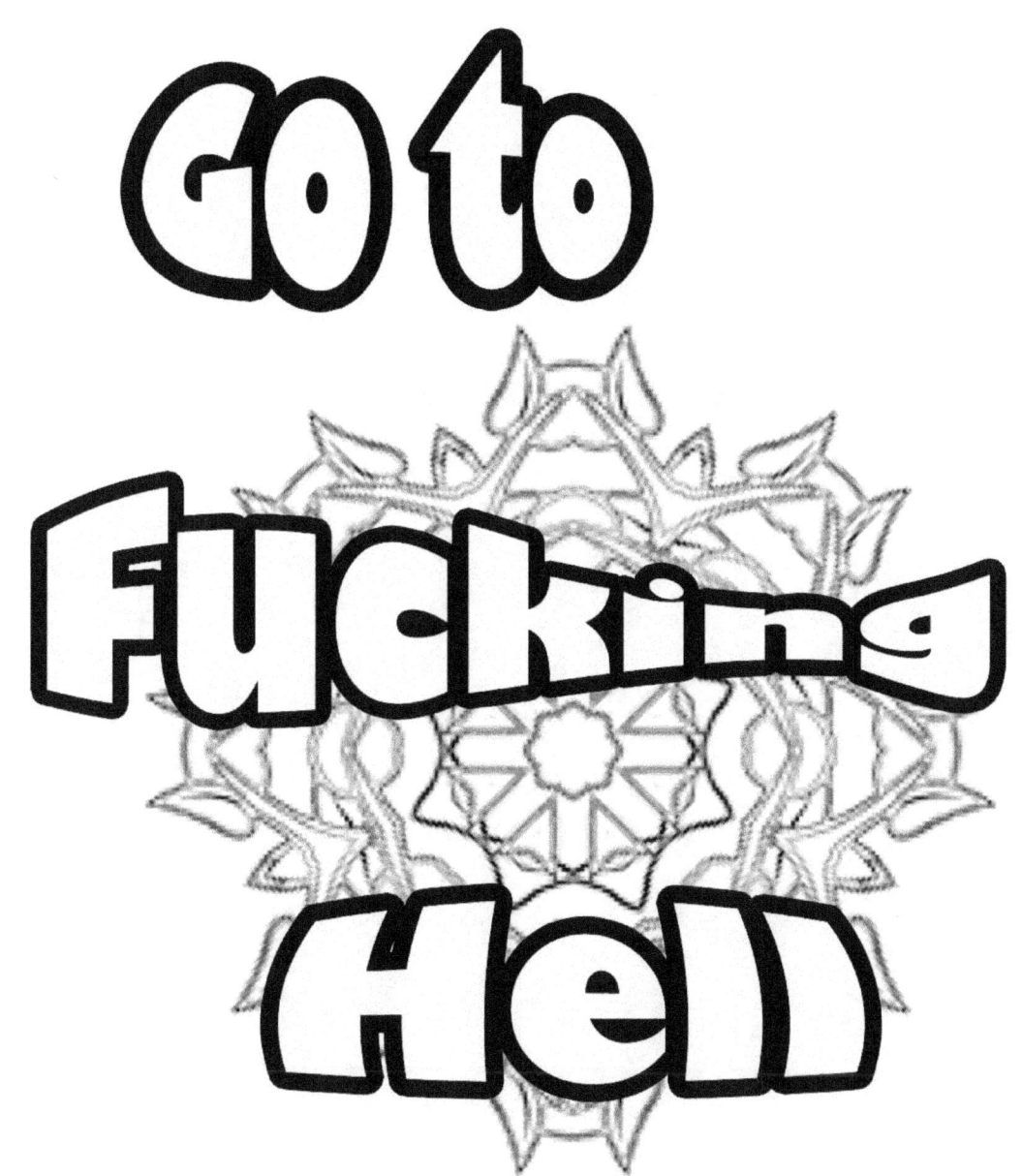

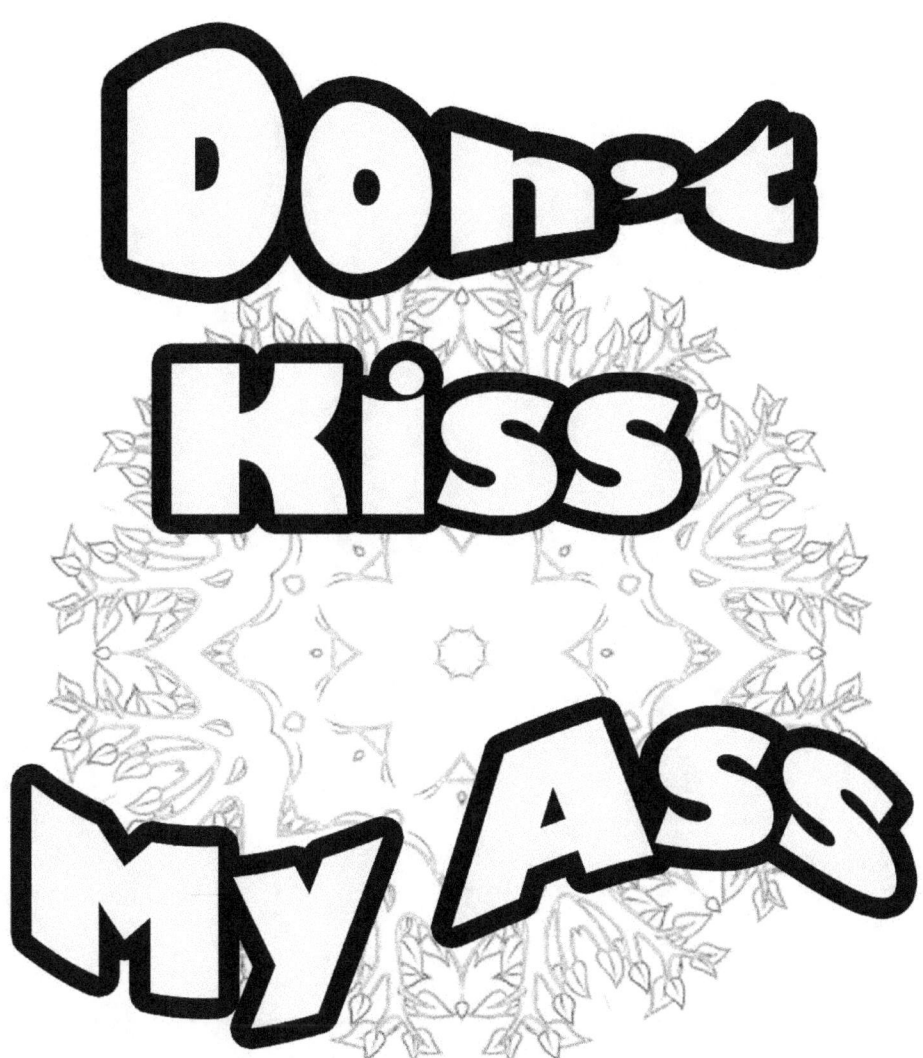

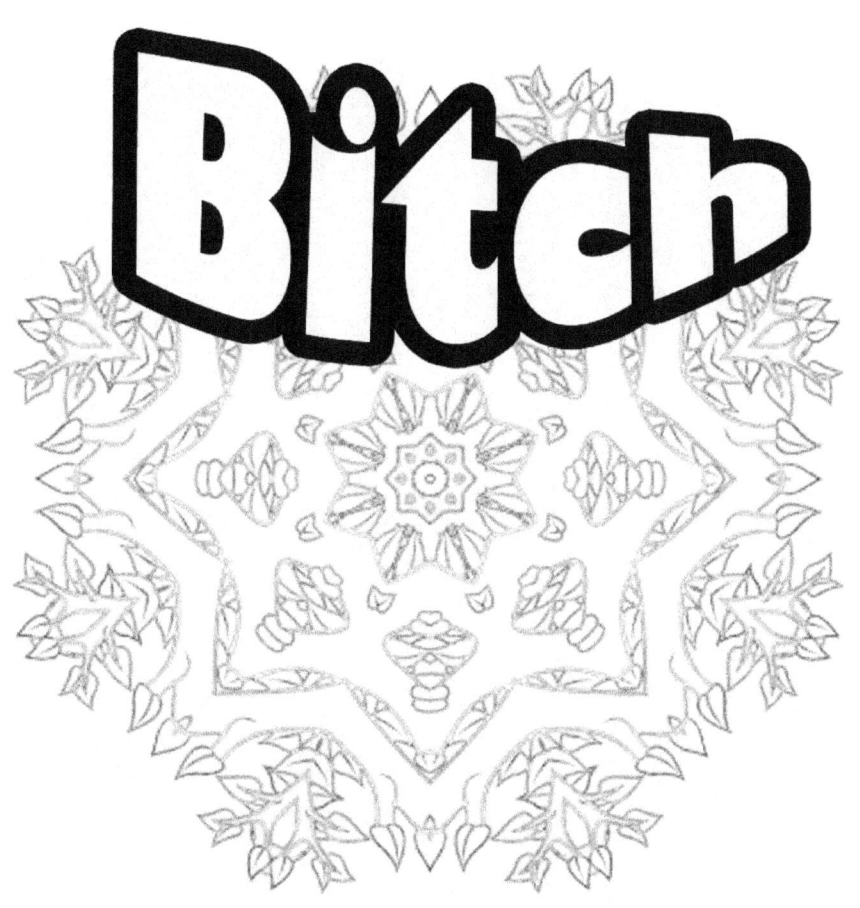

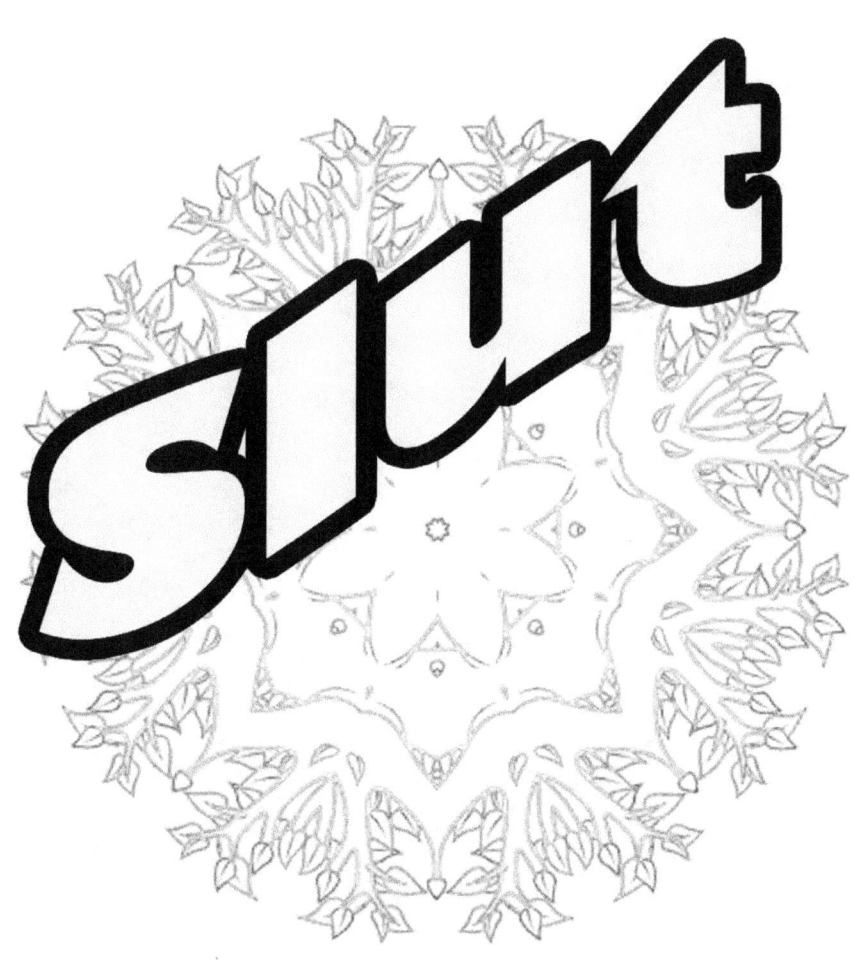

I am in Deep Shit

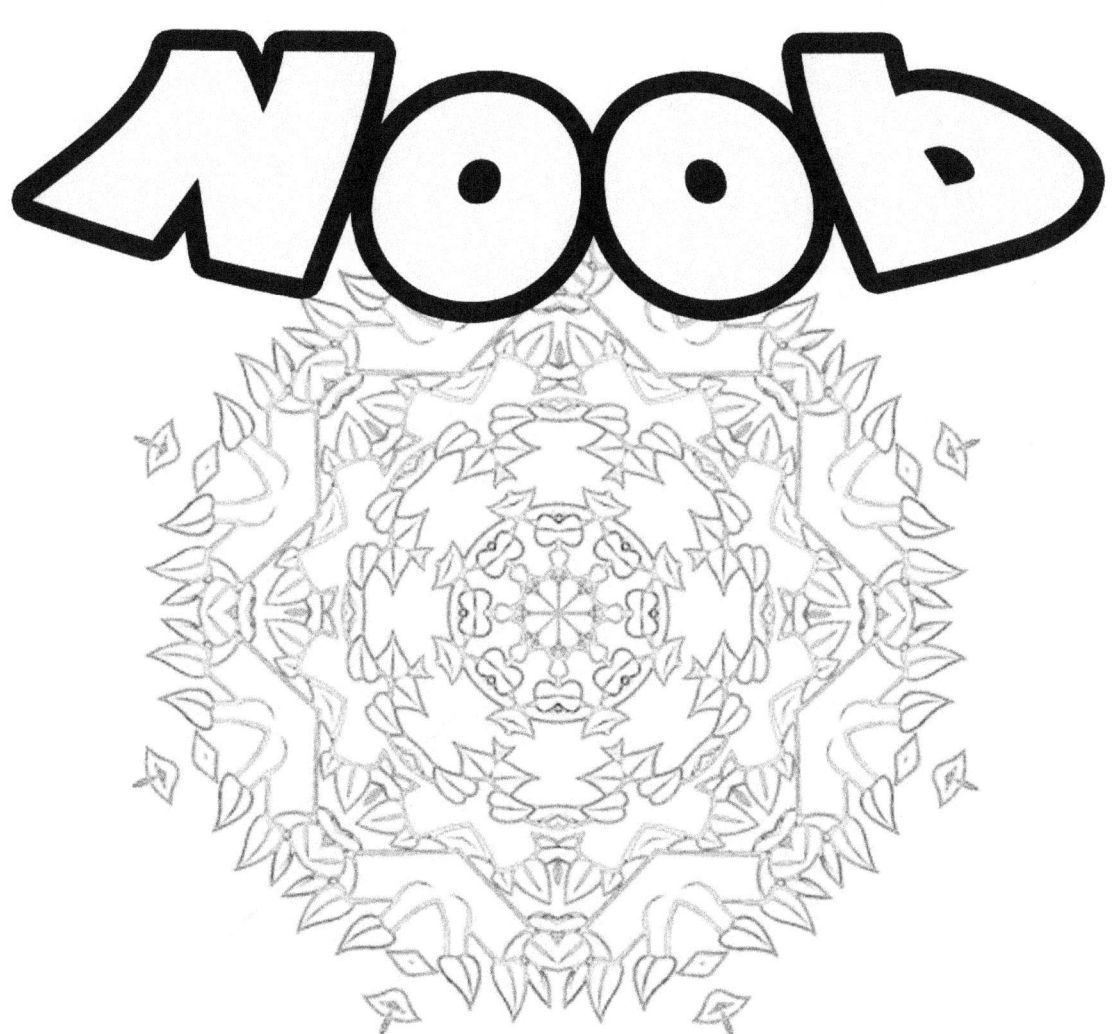

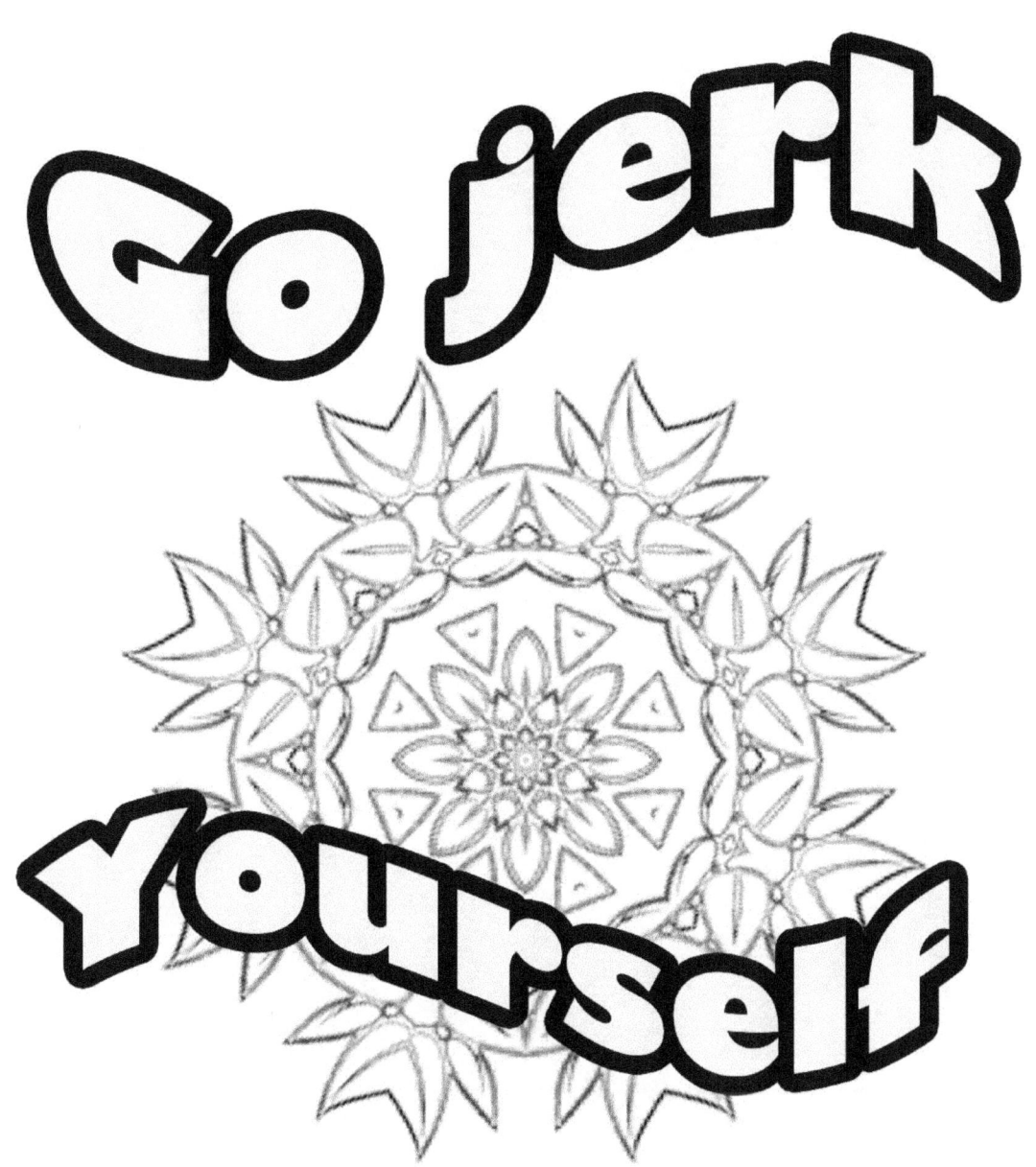

Pervert

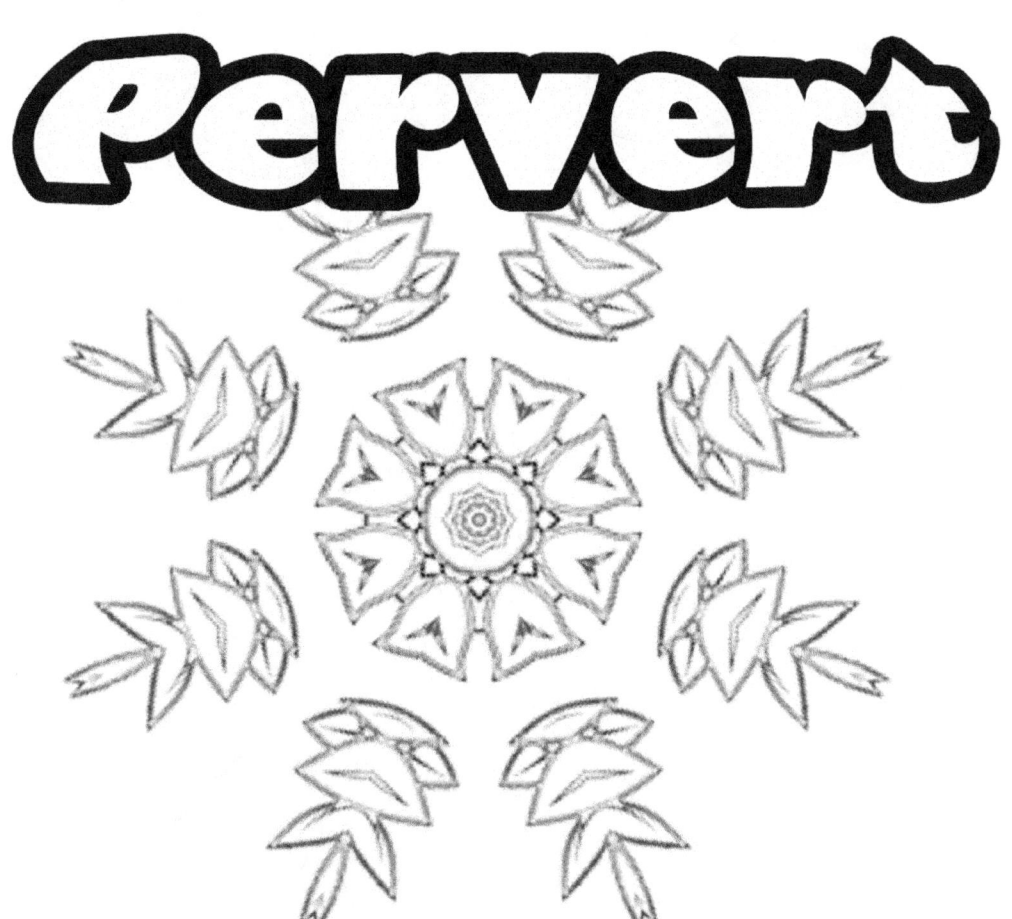

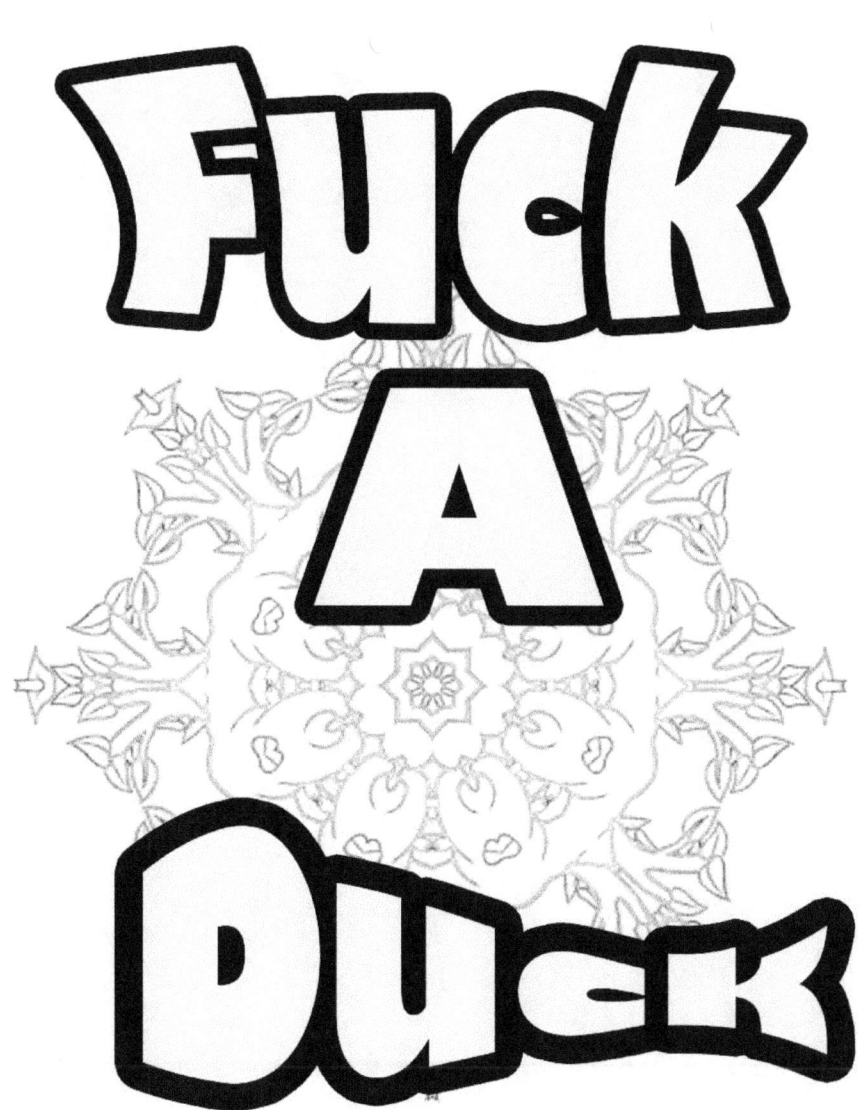

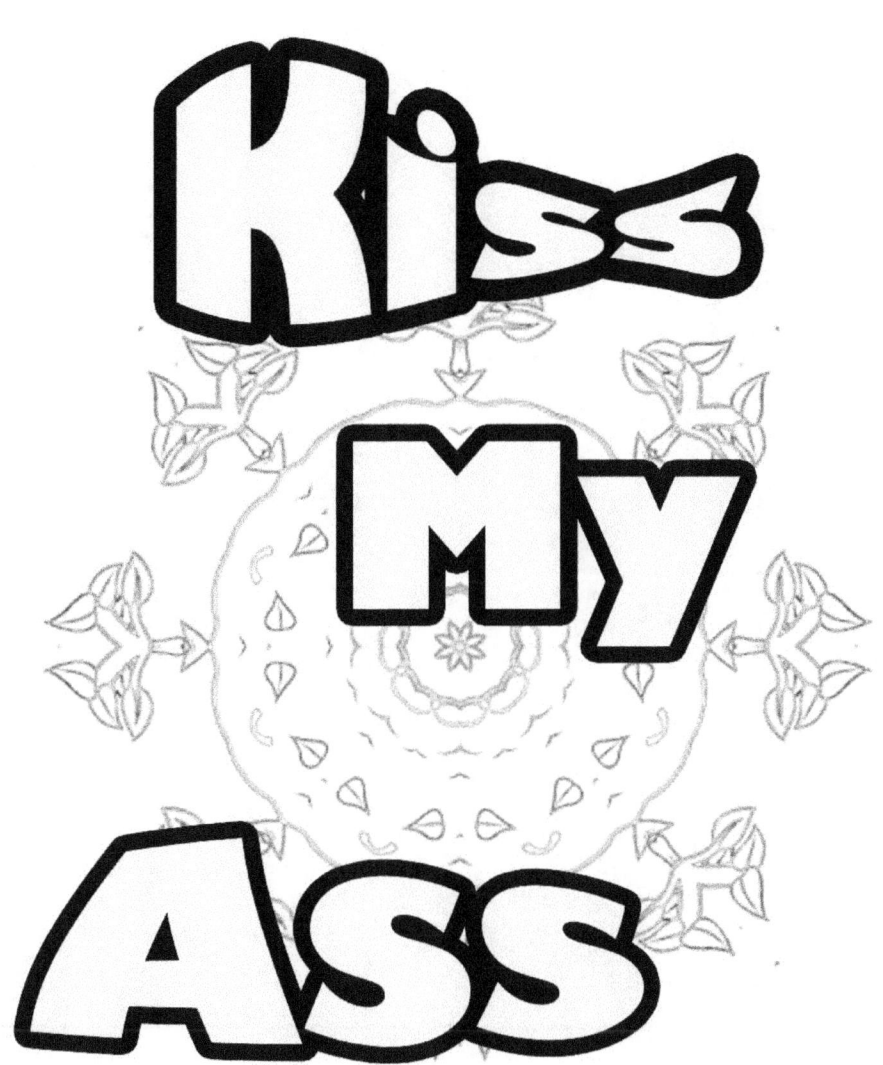

Asshole

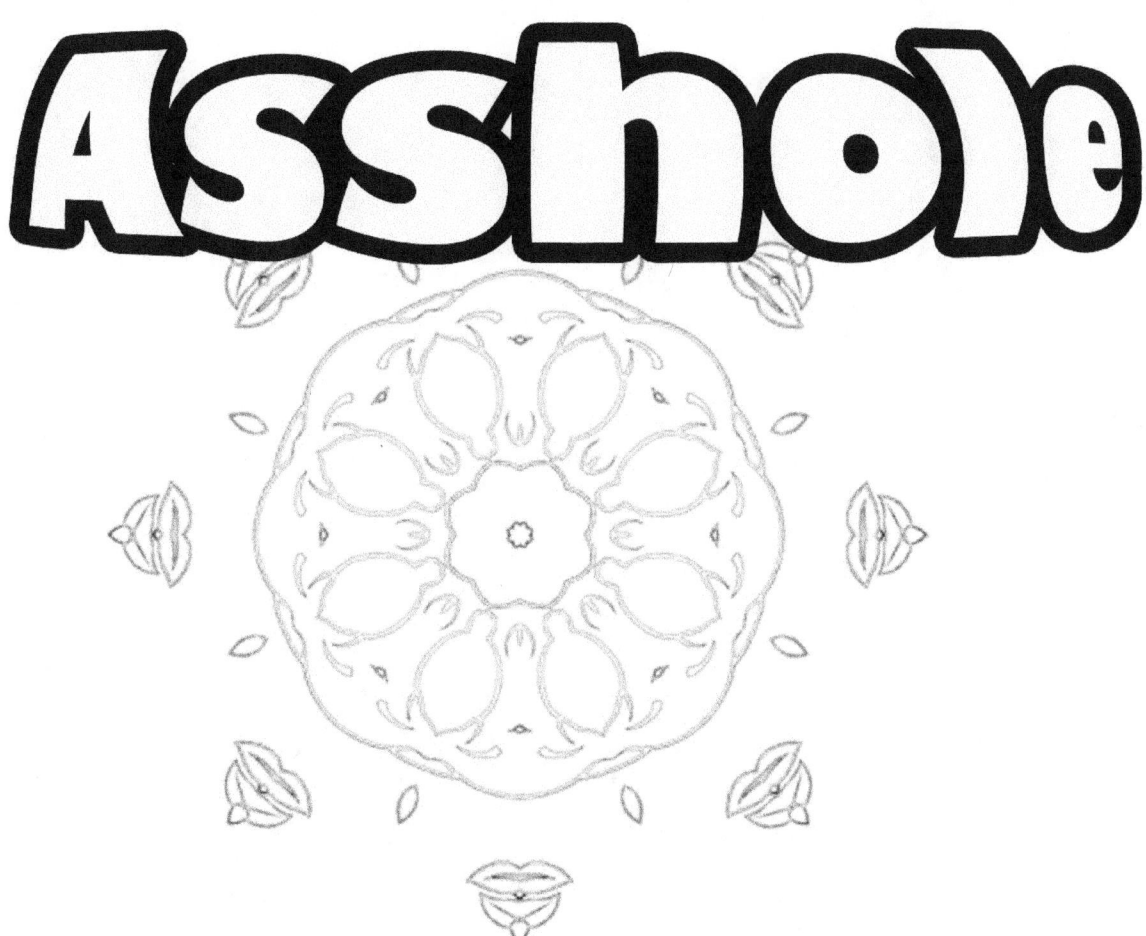

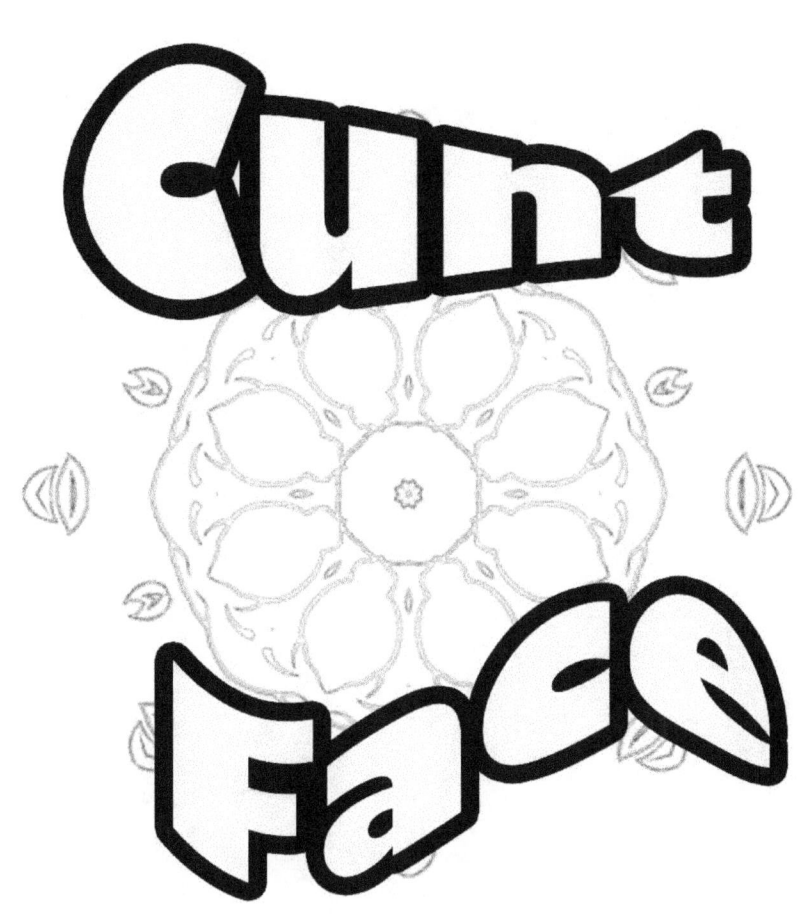

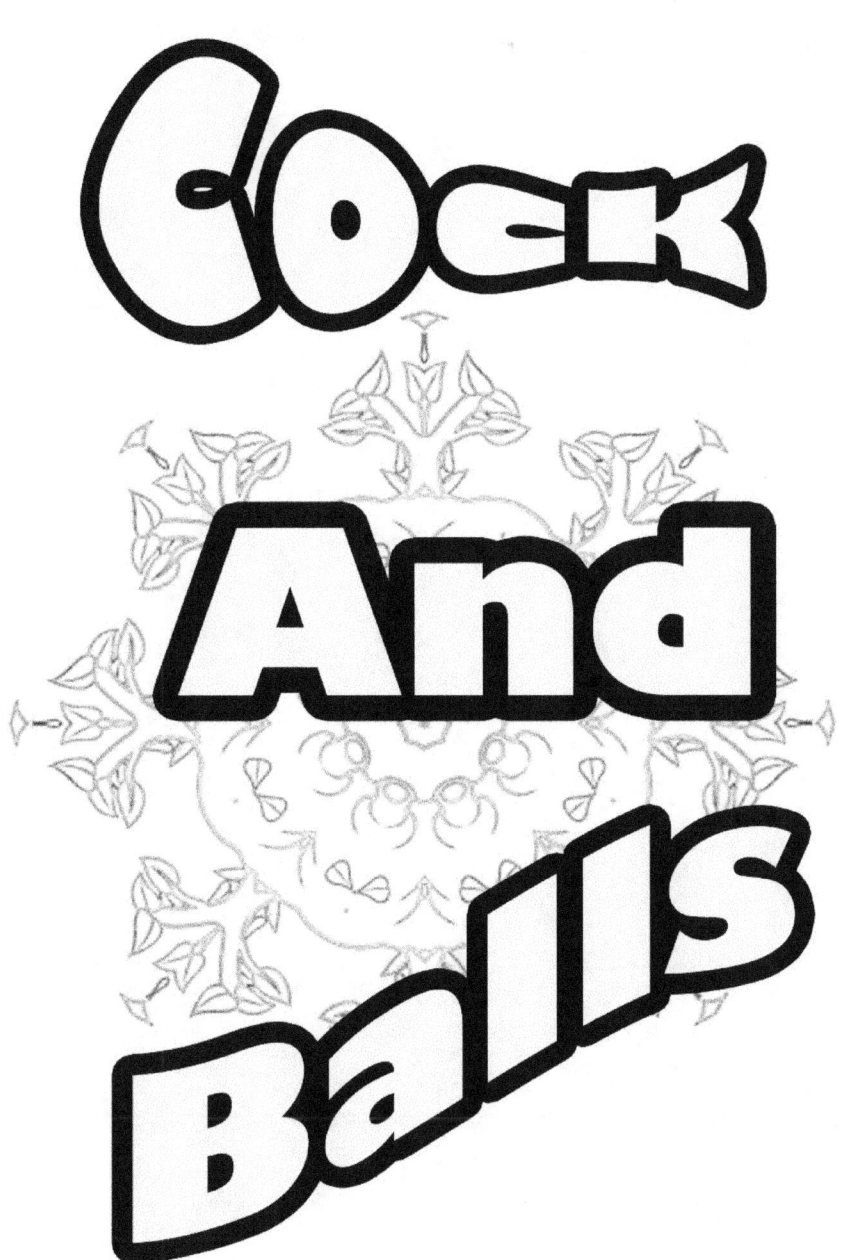

Cock And Balls

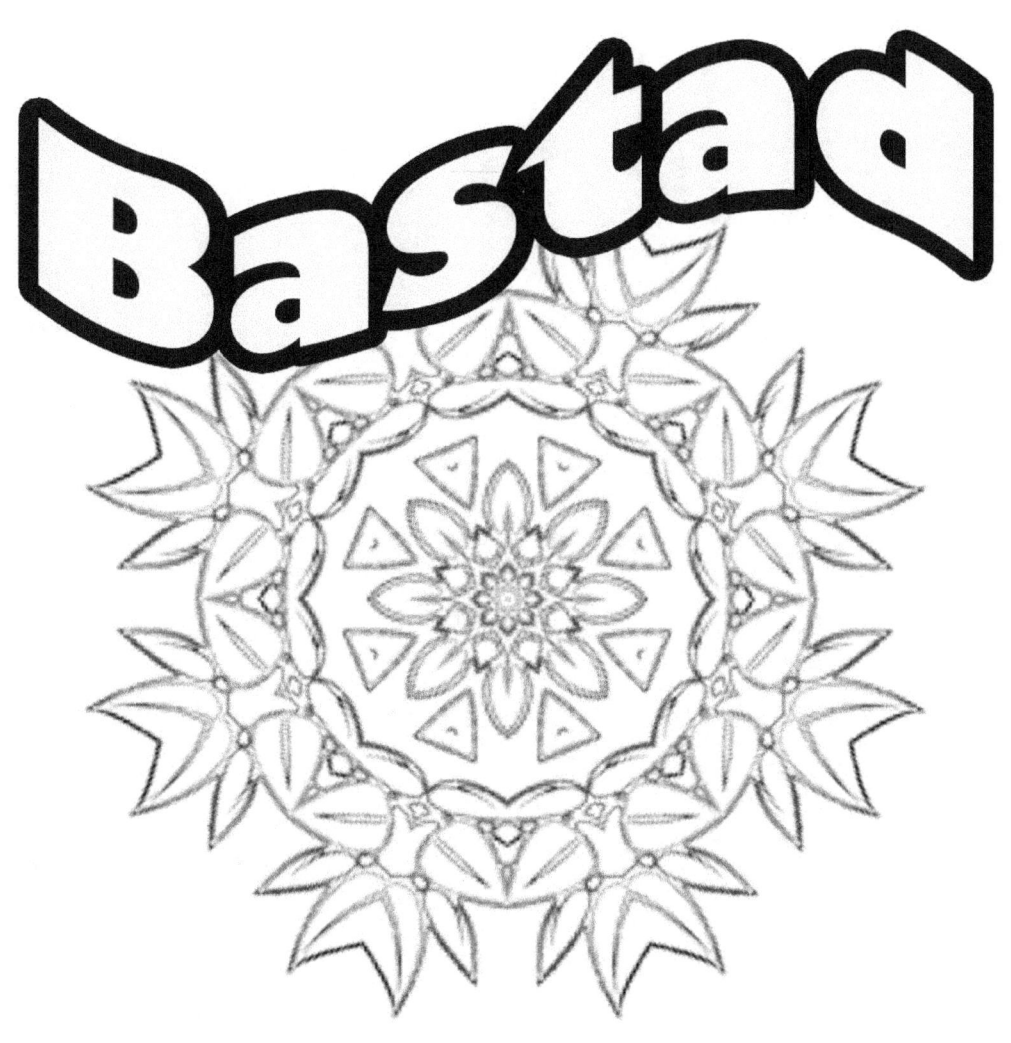

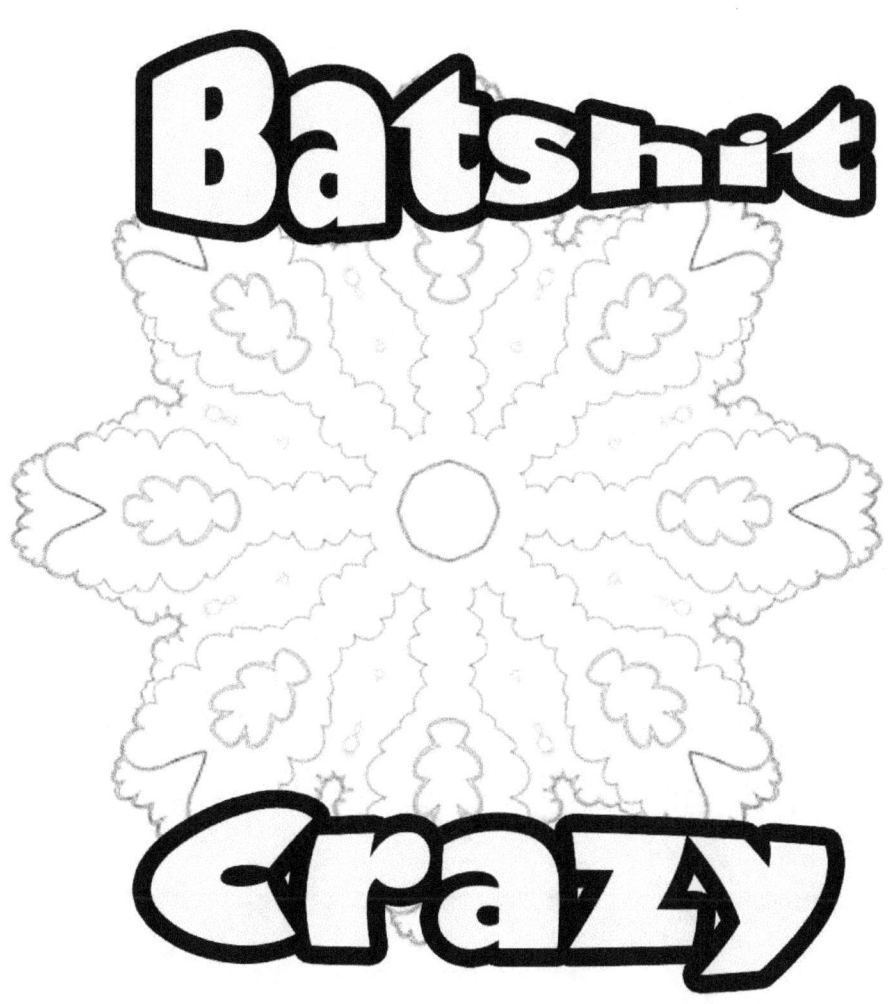

Batshit Crazy

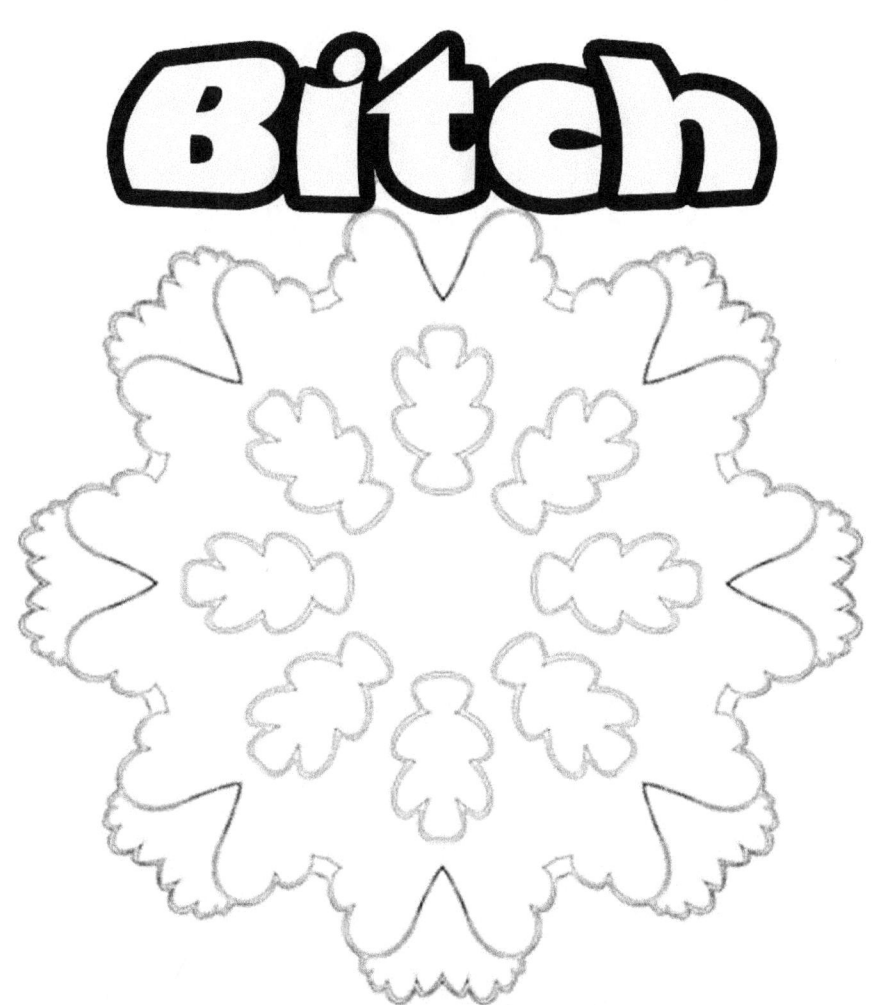

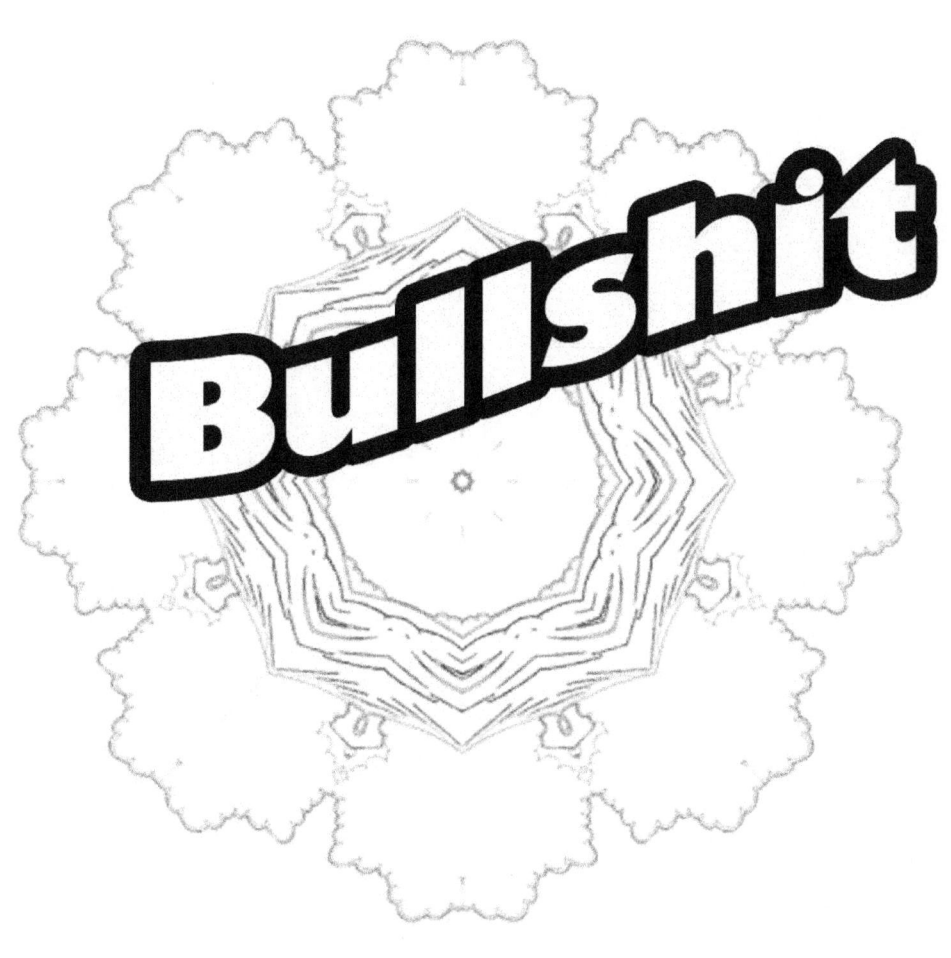

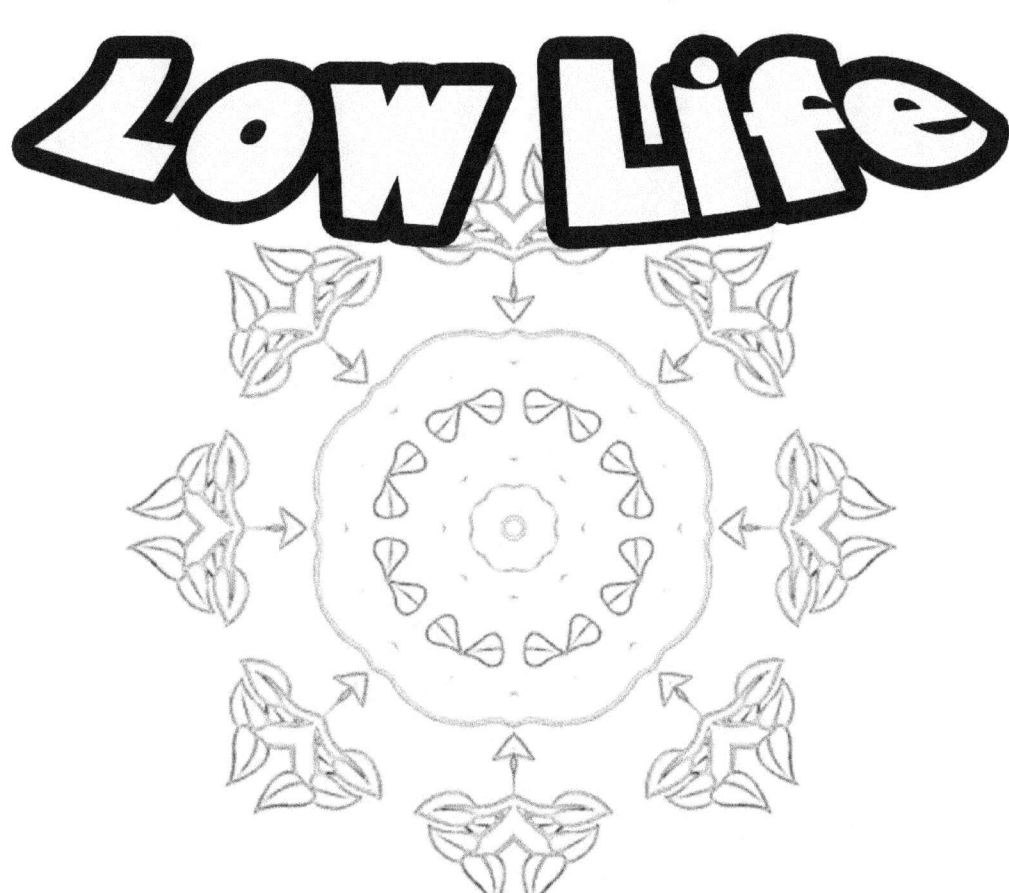

www.ingramcontent.com/pod-product-compliance
Lightning Source LLC
Chambersburg PA
CBHW080641190526
45169CB00009B/3456